Waiting for a Hero

A Breakthrough Book
No. 58

Waiting For a Hero

Poems by
Penelope Austin

University of Missouri Press
Columbia, 1988

University of Missouri Press, Columbia, Missouri 65211
Printed and bound in the United States of America

Library of Congress Cataloging-in-Publication Data
Austin, Penelope.
    Waiting for a hero : poems / by Penelope Austin.
        p. cm.—(A Breakthrough book ; no. 58)
    ISBN 0-8262-0673-5 (alk. paper)
    I. Title. II. Series.
PS3551.U87M9   1988   87-26354
811'.54—dc19   CIP

The publication of this book has been supported by a grant
from the National Endowment for the Arts.

I am grateful to the editors of the magazines in which the
following poems have appeared: *American Poetry Review,*
"Mrs. Walker's Injuction Becomes a Desire" and "How Not
to Die"; *Antioch Review,* "Margaret Hammond December 8,
1916–April 21, 1972" ("Before the Station"); *New Republic,*
"Modernism" and "Going Back"; *Poetry Canada Review,*
"The Unwriting"; *Quarterly West,* "Demolition Derby." I am
also grateful to Mark Strand, Richard Howard, Richard
Schramm, Scott Cairns and Marcia Vanderlip, Kevin Cant-
well and Betsy Lerner, Wyn Cooper, Kathy Fagan and
Stuart Lishan, Ralph Wilson, and L. W. Lucas.

For Alexandra Margaret Austin
and for Jan Engholm
and to all my bad choices

The Devins Award for Poetry

Waiting for a Hero is the 1988 winner of The Devins
Award for Poetry, an annual award originally made
possible by the generosity of Dr. and Mrs. Edward
A. Devins of Kansas City, Missouri. Dr. Devins was
President of the Kansas City Jewish Community
Center and a patron of the Center's American Poets
Series. Upon the death of Dr. Devins in 1974, his
son, Dr. George Devins, acted to continue the
Award.

Nomination for the Award is made by the
University of Missouri Press from those poetry
manuscripts selected by the Press for publication in
a given year.

Contents

I

Modernism

That is not my country, though I speak
as a ghost now. There forever means
forever, and there is no need for dignity
among the souls in the long processional
blurring into sky. Still, even at the fit
end of pain toward which they rode, madly,
maudits, on fast horses, in fast cars,
or unwillingly by the boxcarful,
they turn to one another with what's left:
a single perfect note held unwaveringly.
That is the eternity they believed in.
Their condition is the music of souls
stretching now and forever like the thin skin
of embarrassment they wear for absent bodies
cast off in another country left behind.

Eternal Love

Play it. The line of palms stretching along
    the blue coast, and the train's song
      as it coasts into the station. Play
    it again. Golden grains of couscous

harden where the wine stains
    the tablecloth, beneath the fingernail idly
      scratching at the table beneath stars, stars like
    the grains of golden sand on the beach, golden sand

ground into golden skin. Play it again.
    She's wearing a white dress, of course,
      and sandals. His eyes go from blue to green
    to brown and back again to the sea.

    Oh, the lovers come and go
    across the gilt-edged borders of Morocco.

Penelope's Sonnet

You don't smell of the sea
            tonight. Yet you rush in to me
as if returning from a long voyage,
            with the anchors on your buttons

effaced by your calloused fingers' response
            to the climates; larks have nested
in your beard. I long for a house
            with a widow's walk. Attuned

to the distance I would count
            the sheets coiled on your ship's deck,
assess the rents in your sails,
            calculate the knots between our berths.

You've never shared my passion for the gothic—
so why does your face taste wet and salty?

Lover

Lunatic. Some new world
this is—me still
trudging up the mountain in full sun, past
the potters and the glassblowers, carrying
a straw bag, in sandals, in love, brown legs, sweat.
My Chinese fortune cookie tells me: There's
a star kiss for you under the night sky.
There it is: the sky again, and stars,
the ambiguous set of my lips—kiss
for a star or *from* a star?—Time-
less pucker, pout, into the black
and descending sky. And I

made my first trip to California
at age thirty-three, breathless, thinking
I'd come back from the dead
and so must be entering a new world, going
as far west as I could go,
to the most feminine of states, and the lightest.
Withered grape vines hung
on wire supports: *Fields* of crucifixes!
Palm, olive, cypress,
cypress, olive, palm, as Greek as my name. Six
months later I returned to California, wishing
to become the most shocking
pink oleander on the roadside
in full bloom. Trees drooping with voluptuous
purple plums. And those peaches, melting
in unreasonable heat.
And south of San Francisco the tawny hills opened
their great and lovely thighs to the sea

so as we drove past I blushed to see
the green vegetation curling in the Vs
formed by each pair of frank legs.

Further south we lay the wrong way
on the old quilt on the old bed and were taken
in briefly by the moonlight, as if
we could participate in a small rectangle, pale
page, of the truth stretching out over the orchards,
nothing between us now, motionless, madly
believing in the perpetuity of the moment,
which was really only the past
reaching *back* into forever. Why
must we go forward from that moment? We could
pull up the wounded edges of the past to meet
the unblemished future cleanly, without
a scar. But men are all vain hope
and have nothing to lose to time.

The next day I stood in shade as slender as sorrow
beneath a decaying plum tree and watched
him walking with the children—his son,
my daughter—in the New Orchard. The young
trees came to the children's waists and sunset
immortalized them, his hair the unruly curls
of a sailor as he waved to me
across the centuries.

Cire-Perdu

That sky
rolls in gray each morning, bears down,
flares briefly vermilion, then withdraws into blue,
dispassionate as understanding.
But I keep my eye on the sea
as the tide comes in, trembling,
salt surface breaking
over the white-ringed rocks that define
the Cote d'Azur.

The one city that was mine is built
from sea-soaked rocks, calcareous stone sullied
by time as indifferent as reasons.
Here in the Old City of Nice, the word hello is *bijou*,
dropped in the arteries of La Vieille Ville,
thickened with olive oil, anchovies packed in brine,
bitter black olives steeped in lavender,
sachets of dried roses. Dark turnings
give out at the central market:
cut flowers, dried fruits,
fish gutted in the public fountain.

For every city there is an older city
taken by siege or convenience
and rebuilt over its old stones until it relinquishes
its name—as a woman relinquishes an old love
who holds the world too lightly between them—
Phoenicia, Byzantium, Nike.
So there is something older than love: in my lost city

the sun is hot beyond reason. The sea
spreads out beneath La Vieille Ville,
across the white-ringed stones,
the stones giving in to the sea,
the sea giving in to the tide,
the tide giving in to the moon,
salt, sweat, oil on my skin.

Clytie's Delivery

During the autumnal equinox
    I spent hours in my grandmother's kitchen
smelling dill and saving
    the thousands of seeds

from faded faces of sunflowers.
    My aunts recited a litany
of intimate relations in Assyrian.
    The foreign rhythms

entered me so completely I learned
    the way the sunflower's
petals quiver when touched. They loved
    so well they were lost

to themselves in winter. It was then
    I created a sun and believed
in regeneration.
    It is winter now.

The sun stays behind the locked door
    of the clouds. My head hangs heavily
on my dried-out stalk. Children have picked out
    the hundreds of eyes

I followed you with. They cracked them
    and ate the seeds of all
I've ever seen. Now my face is pocked
    and blank, a moonface

with shriveled petals, once yellow.
    I know you are gazing brazenly
    from behind platinum clouds.
        You think you exist

beyond my imagination. But as you
    walk away, look down at your hands
    that so lately bruised my petals.
        You'll find yellow dust

on the tips of your fingers
    as you try to brush me off.
    Can you imagine
        yourself without me?

Diana's Leg

The season's color was mauve, exactly
the color of a bruise, exactly the color
of Diana's bruise in fact, the year
she worked as a secretary at *Glamour.*
That's *it!* the fashion editors agreed
and repeatedly bashed at her leg with a stapler
to keep the color pure. Suffer
to be beautiful, Diana used to tell me.

Sometimes when the Stolichnaya's gone
and the glass on my desk has run
dry, I think about Diana's leg,
how fine dancing had made it,
how white it was without the bruise
when she sat years later on the lawn,
her leg articulated by moonlight.

For Merrie-Lee Rebillot

The Sleeping Beauty Ballet

The curtain call brings on Aurore's returns.
It wakes the dancer from the dance she learns.
In the village of Biôt the noon sun burns.
Pots take form as the potter's wheel turns.

It wakes the dancer from the dance she learns:
the bouquet of roses holds a hidden spindle.
Pots take form as the potter's wheel turns.
Heat and spinning make long days dwindle.

The bouquet of roses holds a hidden spindle.
The bowing dancer takes the treacherous bouquet.
Heat and spinning make long days dwindle
in fragile figured urns and wine pichets.

The bowing dancer takes the treacherous bouquet.
The curtain falls, the dancer faints in sleep.
In fragile figured urns and wine pichets,
a century collapses in a heap.

The curtain falls, the dancer faints in sleep.
The audience will snore a hundred years.
A century collapses in a heap.
The urns pile up; the potter's in arrears.

The audience will snore a hundred years.
The Prince recalls his Beauty with a kiss.
The urns pile up; the potter's in arrears.
What to do with so many pots as this?

The Prince recalls his Beauty with a kiss.
Sleeping Beauty wakes again to chance.
What to do with so many pots as this,
as common as death, as careful as a dance?

Sleeping Beauty wakes again to chance.
The hidden spindle pricks the art of passion.
As common as death, as careful as a dance,
the potter's art has fallen out of fashion.

The hidden spindle pricks the art of passion.
Love for awakened beauty breaks the trance.
The potter's art has fallen out of fashion
like the lifeless form of beauty in the dance.

Love for awakened beauty breaks the trance
and reinspires beauty's breathless turns.
Like the lifeless form of beauty in the dance,
night's curtain call brings on aurora's returns.

for Tom Schmid

Virginia Woolf's Downstairs Maid on the Occasion of Moving to Monks House, 1939

> "the ghastly business"
> —Virginia Woolf

Considering the lateness of the hour
it's a wonder we're still moving about
these rooms. Only the servants are around.
This is the hour of burglars, rats, drink-drowned
poets, and nursing mothers, of the fire dying out,
the past up in smoke, the shade pulled down
askew, and what's left when the furniture's
gone, the core of our mistress's house

bombed out. If we stayed just a week longer
that young newsagent on the corner . . .
who knows? I can imagine our child with stray
curly hair. My mother will miss me on Sunday.

I walk through these rooms as if the table's *here*,
the divan still *there*. When I open the window, I hear
the city flood in as the shade flaps out. But my ear
obeys the echo of the instructions I received.
I sponge the walls. I don't want to leave
this place, but I'm bound to leave it clean.

Chinese Maps

After we met under the clock in Cho Fu Sa,
we walked back along the towpath,
arms around each other, your hard
hip pressed against mine.

The servants bumped along behind, stubbing
their toes on stones embedded in brown sand.
Those ducks—teals? We hardly noticed
the glinting river

winding home, or the willows alongside it
I shinnied up, murdering ants
between my thighs before my
own blood stained my legs.

When I met you, I told you nothing
of my blisters. I didn't
think of them. When we returned
only I noticed

the gray in your hair and I swear
you looked the philosopher grown old
in those strange lands without me,
with other women,

perhaps. Your absence had become
so much a presence to me, it was
your leanness that reminded
me of what I missed:

You peeling the layers of clothing off me,
jacket, vest, blouse, unbraiding
my hair. I pull it back now, no bangs
across my forehead,

streaks of white. The pile of clothing grew
like the weakness of desire, like years . . .
Tonight I lift your arm
from across my neck

and slip into the room where I've watched you
working, or shrugging your arms
into your embroidered jacket, explorer,
to leave me again.

Your maps are stretched across the table,
the boxes drawn within boxes. I trace
their colors, your direction, with my finger.
I rename countries

with the years of my life. Here
I was a child, here I took my hair down,
here I turned my face to the wall, here
you returned. Farther

and farther from the center the boxes grow
all the way to the new world. I looked
it up today: time is masculine;
love is feminine.

You might trust me, since I wrote
to you in my own blood, and you
spoke to me in Mandarin
for the longest time.

When Is a—

When she is in a hospital bed,
for example. Let's say

both her breasts have just been
cut off. She leaves her husband.

—woman—

He says you can paint a trashcan,
but it's still a trashcan.

For months she cannot raise her arms
to hold them open for her child.

She drives cross-country. Her wounds
are dressed along the way.

She builds bookcases.
She hangs pictures.

She takes out the trash.
A lover leaves her for a young woman

—not a—

who has no breasts or kids to begin with.
He says no one wants to hear

what you have to say. She reads
the history of men's poetry.

She drinks like a man. Then cortisone
makes her shoulders grow big as a ferryman's.

She begins to lose her hair, her eyelashes,
The ocean in her dries up, and she

can no longer bleed. She is tired
all the time. She goes to bed.

                                        —woman?

She is alone, abed, early. In the morning,
her daughter crawls into her bed,

into her arms, and wakes her, calls her
by her woman's name.

The Silent Woman

Elle vit apparaître le matin
Elle se tut discrètement
—from the lithograph "1001 Nights"
by Henri Matisse

Scheherazade's one who was able to master
the art of telling stories to save her life,
spinning until morning to avert disaster.

A thousand and one times enraptured, her jailer
laid aside his jewel-encrusted knife
as the artful woman became his fancy's master.

She couldn't allow her charming voice to falter
until it broke finally into Arabian light
that returned her each morning without disaster.

Then did she dream of a woman who passed *her*
nights unweaving a day's work, an art that died
silently with the return of her able master?

In the end the fascinated king clasped her
to him and made her his tale-spinning wife.
From then on mornings appeared without disaster.

I wonder if she continued to tell stories after
she began sleeping unveiled with her husband at night.
The one art a woman must be able to master
is spinning till morning to avert disaster.

What She Weaves

I know time like the back of my hand:
                    the knuckles on my fist, blue

veins, two small dark spots. And I know
                    truth like the key I turn

in the door of our empty house, a key
                    presuming a lock. But what there is

is ineradicable waiting—though
                    Telemachus is no dream, no

ghost, not a doll I learn to dress,
                    no statue with faded paint

for eyes, no, a man like Odysseus, the boy
                    as lost to memory as his birth,

so only the joy, then the boy,
                    then the man remains. No,

I would not stop him, not because I couldn't—
                    whose face do you think

I've been weaving here in bright colors
                    while my hair turns gray?

Yes, I tear it apart each night,
                    not to stop time in faith

that Odysseus will return,
                    but to let Telemachus' face

alter in the sea-wind blowing constantly
                    against him. And should Odysseus

return—? What I know
                    is the art of waiting.

Truth is waiting
                    is hard, but that's life.

And where there's life—
                    Telemachus, not Odysseus.

The return of the shuttle.
                    The return of the shuttle.

II

Going Back

Gypsies came down my street in summer
    and spilled their satin ribbons, gaudy beads,
  and yards of scarves and brightly colored

remnants on the boulevard. We swarmed
    around, holding our bats and butterfly
  nets, drawn to the exotic perfume

of distant countries. Our mothers
    slipped out from behind screen doors
  and came to stand behind us, arms

around our shoulders, palms of their hands
    pressed flat against our chests, drawing
  us close against their legs. And in the late

dry breeze of August, the iceman
    heaved blocks as cold as the memory
  of winter on his tattooed shoulder. The ragman

and the scissors-grinder sang their way
    along our street. On other days
  the organ-grinder danced with his monkey

and a man with a pony photographed
    each of us in front of the houses we left.
  All this happened in the warm season

when one sweet day rolled after another
    before memory gave us something to hope for.
  Now I can't say for sure that the gypsies

came down my street more than once, though
    these days I remember waiting for them,
  as if at thirty-five, entering every city

a stranger, I could turn my feet to the past
    and still find something coming toward me,
  something whose shape I know.

There is no art to wandering.

Mrs. Walker's Injunction Becomes a Desire

At Daisy's age I was initiated by an Italian
in the backseat of a Fiat. I'd begun to walk
to *il centro di Roma,* a sultry hour
away, naively oblivious to the unhealthy
urbanity of the city I'd sauntered off
to find. The blurred edges of Rome were beautiful,

but I was pursuing the clearly beautiful:
deep catacombs, curlicue friezes, Italian
inlaid marbles, and a more ancient sun's glance off
the bleached porticoes of a cloister's walk.
I abandoned my friends, who'd consumed unhealthy
pale *gelati* after a golden noon hour;

mapless, I attempted the Sistine in an hour.
The three *ragazzi* in the car were beautiful
in my estimation, with nothing unhealthy
in their flourish of inviting gestures or their Italian
colloquialisms. Why should I walk?
I accepted the ride, and the driver took off.

The boy in back went right to taking off
my dress, working the silver zipper for a Roman hour.
The "Wedding Cake" glinted on the other side of a walk.
As from under marble his whisper slid: *Com' è bella!*
Even I understood this sliver of Italian.
They say the air above the Tiber is as unhealthy

as the silver age of an empire is unhealthy.
Marble arms, more graceful than strong, fall off
or grow too languid to resist an Italian.
The Pantheon closed its doors during the hour
that Rome fell submissively under the beautiful
certainty of the hot sun slanting up the sidewalk

like a hand sculpting legs too weak to walk.
The Italians must have found my breathing unhealthy;
they dropped me at the Coliseum with a few beautiful
bending over backward kisses and drove off
in the bloom and perfume of Rome. Since that hour
I have desired everything Italian.

Faintly between the lines James wrote: "Walk off
to the Pincio, Daisy. Desire has but one unhealthy hour.
You are beautiful and . . ." The rest is in Italian.

Cloverleaf Somewhere West of Detroit

Remember those acres of new
        unsold cars hot
off assembly waiting
in lots where laid-off employees
    once parked in the bare stripping

wind of November? In the old days
        the changing lights
on the billboard outside
the Chrysler plant steadily clicked off
    each car rolling out. And remember

the giant tire towering over the freeway?
        And the ache of the unfolding
longing for the road, the long sway
of freeway heading west. And always
    after the dozen exit signs

somewhere west of Detroit
        the cloverleaf
you can get off on, continue
on, head in the opposite direction
    to nowhere or arc back on again—

as though the interstate must remind us
        of the interdependence
one heart travels on toward another,
as if it's the heart that carries us
    through salt and ice.

                for Wyn Cooper

What Is So Beautiful

> as a road?
> —George Sand

I wondered how George Sand made her escape
as I sat belted beside you while you
    drove us south on I-75
        past exits we knew by heart. The name
        of every freeway town

defined the set of your jaw, the extension
of your fingers on the steering wheel:
    New Baltimore—a short stack of pancakes;
        Knoxville—chilidogs at four a.m., just
        at the edge of the snowline.

Jonesboro—you were refused spark plugs
because your hair hung below your shoulders
    and it was 1971;
        McDonough—walking through an orchard
        of decaying pecan trees with our daughter;

Cordele—a Chinese restaurant;
Valdosta—alone
    in a Holiday Inn in a hurricane
        while you remained in the Bahamas.
        We drive this road without surprise,

accustomed to the dust. Once
we stopped only in towns with women's names:
    Anna, Ada, Sadieville, Lily, Roberta.
        Though we never go more than a mile
        off the freeway, roads lengthen

past the shack where an old couple
snaps beans on the porch, where a man
    carries a rusty muffler to a scrap-pile
        beside the chicken coop, crossing
        the bare patch of yard in front of a house

sagging against Spanish moss, kudzu,
and brambles. The sleeveless dress
    of a pregnant woman probably slides
        off her shoulder as she reaches to swat
        a kid or a fly. The local old men, trousers

unzipped or slipping down their hips,
sit on stoops in towns so small
    they make you tender. I know these are not
        exits. Yet every time we drive this route,
        I imagine I am a young girl here in the dust

going to town, not beautiful, without choices.
The magnolias that line the road
    would mean nothing to me. But magnolias
        grew beyond the windows of So'n Vent
        on the side that gave out to the sea,

where Aurore Dupin lived with Chopin.
Having already left her name, she left Paris
    on the morning of December 18, 1838,
        pursuing what I would have no imagination for,
        if I were that young girl slipping out

of an old print dress for the son of the man
carrying rusty parts to the scrap-pile, crossing
    the distance to the chicken coop beside
        the road you never drive me along, baron,
        virtuoso, figment of my imagination.

Before the Station

In memory of Margaret Hammond,
December 8, 1916–April 21, 1972

Did I call you Margaret or

did I say nothing to your
back as you leaned against me,
modest even in madness,
so that I could help you dress?
I don't remember the name
I used, but how you trusted
me to support your greater
weight as you maneuvered one

foot into a torn stocking,
apologizing for its
age, for your deflated breasts,
sagging skin, yellowed toenails.
I had been told that once you
were beautiful, but that day
I was made the sole keeper
of your modesty, the last

remnant of your sanity.
I dressed you in the last gown
that you ever wore, and as
I fastened the tie and smoothed
away the white strands of hair
from your face, I filled the last
space in your memory. When
you died you were much smaller

than I remembered, smaller
than I am. Six pallbearers
carried you effortlessly.
Your son was not one of them.
He looked out at the spring fields
passing by the funeral car,
examined the machinery
of the grave hoist, held his face

in the exact expression

of the seventeen-year-old
in the photograph you kept
by your bed. Once you told me:
you should meet my son. You
wondered where he was while he
waited outside your room for
me, not saying I am your
son because he was your son,

and you had no room for him
when he approached your bedside,
a man, not the boy who so
quickly outgrew the shirts that
you buttoned for him, reaching
around his shoulders as he
leaned back against your fine legs.
New grass and small wildflowers

rise from your untended grave,
but you don't remember them.
The granddaughter you never
dreamed possible is growing
into your name, but you don't
remember her. Your son now
begins to forget the names
of recent acquaintances,

remembering only old
gestures, pushing our daughter's
small shoulders around, bending
double over her to pull
on her socks as she supports
herself against his knees. If
memory is the key to
immortality, then I

fear language, its power to

compose each new memory
in seven-syllable lines.
If you died because you had
no more room for memories,
I fear feeling your son's breath
in my hair, seeing ice break
in winter, smelling autumn.
But one memory persists:

a woman shaped in sandstone,
nameless, barefoot, balancing
a stone pitcher on her head,
naked to the hips, belly
swollen with the small body
of water given every
woman at birth, one smooth thigh
immodestly thrusting through

the folds of her skirts as she
leans forward across the stones
that the Grecians used to build
Antibes and Nice, stones trampled
by Napoleon's boots, stones
that form the crypts of dead fish
and fishermen washed up from
the sea. Once I thought a kiss

was a passport to truth, that
a dance was a glimpse into
infinity, that a sigh
was the precise sound of one
clean angle of the shape of
all sound so that once I thought
I touched immortality.
But we are flesh, contained in

tender skin. I would call you

back. I would show you the sand-
stone woman standing before
the Gare de Biôt. Margaret,
she collects weather in her
eyes, nose, lips, and ears because
all the crevices of her
body are sealed. The woman
is immortal, balancing.

Waking

In the small space
of early morning, regrets
are quiet, the retracted criteria
of the world as it sleeps away pain, curled
in a tight ball beneath my stomach.

Before I have completely
woken to the full brunt
of frail contingencies—barstools
emptying out around me the night before,
the monthly mourning for unborn children,

the hidden promise
in the words *giving up* and *leaving*,
the necessity of giving back
to the world its words *peace* and *freedom*—
I am too small to think about dirt and pain,

and I lie naked,
simply, tangled in sleep
heaped on the bed like an old gown
cleared out of the attic and paraded
before a mirror by my small daughter,

like gauze on wounds
that never heal, nor bleed,
nor flower like the wounds in earth
where seeds are planted and sealed,
wounds more like the regret

that the orange petals
of the jackfruit's flesh are not flowers,
        or that I won't remember my past
or that I will. Waking slowly
        I watch the promise of the morning

                turn to gray, diffuse,
flatten the earth the way that you
        have become my regret as it finally
dawns on me fully: I won't be leaving
        or even tracing new routes in the fine lines

                now appearing in your face.

Never *he said say jungle again*

Though all around was waste and wild,
though jewel beetles gleamed from the undersides of leaves,
and monkeys cried out in two syllables.

Vipers wound round the posts of the plank road at ankle
    height,
so I hardly dared look through the light arcing
on my lashes to the tangle of leaves

at the dome of trees, or beyond
the speckled patterns of leaf shadows and dark
animal forms on limbs made strong under their weight.

I hardly dared breathe or listen to the fear at least
half desire pulsing in my ears, or part my lips, dry
cracked betrayers of a moist interior where the wrong word

kept forming in the mucus at the back of my throat,
footsteps, beetles, bird calls . . .
two beats.

We came suddenly to a door that blocked the path
a mile from the cave, closed, padlocked, jamb flanked
and overtopped by wild vegetation, vines draped

across it, cracks encrusted with moss and gray-green mold.
We could step down off the plank road, swing
off its railings, into the bottomless green

surge of undergrowth, wade through the tangle of vipers
and vines, and bypass the door, hand
on a heart, perhaps,

this absurd door!—
as if the rotting frame could disarm
crimson flowers, blue frogs, monkey calls,

the iridescent butterflies called Rajah Brookes,
and the dank smell of the wet clay walls
of the cave lying somewhere beyond.

He has a photograph of me standing on this side
of the door, brown as a native, eyes shocked
by the flash, hair a tangle, fingers curled

in the vines. It was taken the split second
before I discovered the lock was not fast,
before I pushed through, crossed the threshold.

Leavetaking

I must leave today.
                    I fold my clothes and
    lay them in my suitcase as if this were
your first birth. I watch from the window as

your graceless fingers slit a milkweed pod
    to extract the promise of next summer.
Today as I watch your small obstetric,

I recall why the milkweed folds its
    leaves into its roots and dies as you walk
away with your prize.
                    I know the rough touch

of hands pulling back the resistant skin
    of milkweed cases, of foreign fingers
cutting back the folds of the deepest wound.

I can remember the heart's downward rush
    to appeal against your childish desire
to leave, its plea,
                    Don't abandon me.

You see, this is not our first leavetaking,
    and I would have kept you holed up beneath
my heart forever had you not chosen

to desert me. This is the day the mare
    goes off to the Sweepstakes, the day the milk-
weed reappears in a distant city,

a day of early spring abandon. You
   know I fear your milkweed desire to burst
into wind, guiltlessly.
                              Give me this day

to study my strength, to teach the vengeful
   selfishness of desertion, this one day
to nurture in you the milkweed seeds of

despair. You will make your next leave gentler,
   our next reunion the violent cleaving
of the heart's knowledge to the future,

my silk-haired milkweed seed, my physician.

                              for my daughter

Attachments

As my hands take the steering wheel, I think
of the complex musculature that connects
the hand to the brain, of the intricacy

of nerves twisted around the spinal chord's
center, the gelatinous locus of impulse
and reaction that two people know nothing of

and that can't be repaired. Here in the midwest
the landscape is three-quarters sky, and
driving south, I see the road ahead disappear

into a scrim of rising heat so thin
I am forever driving into sky. Lying immobile,
my father hears voices from the other side,

his mother and brother calling his name,
as if his name can still apply. In the morning,
he wills his hands to move, and with great effort

touches his thumb to the forefinger of his large
left hand grown gaunt and mottled like farmland
seen from a sudden rise in the road. When

my father's head falls back, and I have placed
a cold cloth over his eyes and forehead,
I stroke his arm, massage his fingers. Catching

the sound of my skin on his shoulder
he asks if I am holding his hand. I never say
yes, as if there is some connection between

the place I touch and truth. I have no
imagination and rarely dream, but sometimes
sitting on the floor beside my father I think I know

something of what he is feeling when he wakes
believing his body is a contingency, only to find
himself weighted to a bed of water, air continually

blowing around him to keep his skin tough, to keep
it from dissolving. I know something
of the body's indifferent insistence on the immediate.

Last night, spent, still feeling the ridges
of the road beating miles beneath me, I fell
asleep deeply during an embrace.

Fall in the West

God, what a day. 10-hour
   drive across the West in my Renault,
   Wyoming like a Watteau,
so I think of French
        horsethieves. And coming

through the tunnel that opens on
   Green River, of your mother giving birth
   on this anniversary of the day ether was
used for the first time,
       and *The Magic Flute*

was first performed, the first man was executed
   in this country, back east, and James Dean
   died in a car crash. All that
seems appropriate
       somehow, as I smoke

the cigarettes you left in the car, thinking
   you would travel with me. Christ,
   although before I turned fifteen
I thought I could be
       Theresa, Jesus

never received such thoughts from me.
   But then, I've heard that Mary felt
   no pain at birth, and so withheld
no thoughts for herself—
       which is why women

love men more, knowing precisely
   how much space another woman
   has left unloved in her child. So
I drive 80 through
         Wyoming, risking

heaven in the assurance of the sun
   on my thighs that might as well be
   your hand, the wind on my neck your laughter
as God's though I know
         you think less of me.

Demolition Derby

That summer we claimed iced shots,
the Blue Note, hot nights, hard rock,
the first taste of coffee, acrid
as anonymity. We tried to add

the demolition derby, but in the slow heats,
the engines spewed orange smoke smelling
of ginger, obscuring the destruction
of already ruined bodies—the Mustang,

the Chevette, the Gran Torino—so
the collisions were unimportant.
That summer the heat claimed
forty-four lives, mostly old women

who had no fans, who shut their windows
and forgot to take off old gray sweaters,
or nightgowns with frayed cuffs and flannel
rubbed off, leaving a transparent net

that exposed white flanks lined with blue
and flecked with heat sores. No one
much cared, for it's not the climate
that changes. For example, a century ago

another old woman, celebrated for the purity
of her skin stretched like the unwrinkled
distance between beauty and notoriety, injected
small doses of arsenic distilled by fire

on a flat tile of white porcelain. She found
only that what saves destroys. Her face
collapsed like time before she died.
I think she didn't leave her house

or even approach windows. She quietly
fanned the creases of her face, streaking
the rouge she applied alone, not
knowing the antidotes: coffee, alcohol, heat.

A Last Poem for Alexandra, from the Old Country

Sweet World of Love
my daughter calls me from her bed. I steel
my heart against her, tell her to sleep,

and close the door against the irony.
Sweet World of Love! Today
I learned that love is practically lost

to our vocabulary; time has worn
down its impractical lace jabots, small
gold clasps at the cuffs—time wearing

the galvanized armor of history shields
the little silk underthings washed only by hand
and pinned to a line

in the garden, bravely waving in the wind, waving
to the train heading to Lausanne, Paris, Pittsburgh,
its windows dotted with the flowered babushkas

of washerwomen who look down at their reddened
hands lying in their laps while they practice
the new language:

Chemin de fer.

Good-bye. Good-bye.
Splendid among the cherry blossoms.

for my daughter and
my grandmother

III

The Unwriting

Unpack your suitcase. Unfold
your clothes. Put them on
because the body's something
we can hold, unlike
the country it opens into
where bright fires burning on the frozen lake
reverse a cold heaven
and fishermen in embroidered coats
draw up whitefish on silver lines
from the darkness below the ice.
Close the doors against that scene,
seal them up. Go for a walk
and record the bare branches,
the icicles melting in the sun,
the traffic, the litter,
the derelict bodies hunched
against the cold. And if

you should come to the edge
of Lake Ontario one night in winter
and feel drawn to the fishermen
talking quietly beside ice fires,
remember they'll vanish with winter
like your reflection in the arc of light
on ice, wrapped in layers of warm clothing.
Pull the fur collar up closer
around your neck. Turn back
to the road—where the broken white
line of your voice
is the only sound you hear
after the water settles back
under the ice when the last fish
has been pulled up, gasping.

Plainly

Now the yellowing leaves cling to branches
the way men cling to women in this season

when, they say, men need women most.
The trees reach their branches to the wind

that hears no more than trees can speak.
Although branches break like bones in storms,

this is all metaphorical.
For trees cannot acquire the habit

of hiding the truth as I have
so only a few listening intently

fall so far between the lines
they find the meaning plain.

I want to speak plainly. You see,
once a week I watch a lab technician

draw the blood I've made brothers with
from my one good arm. Then I watch

a doctor shoot an innocent liquid back in.
At first it mixes with a little blood

that tries to get away, then both
disappear into my arm and another

yellow liquid is pumped in. The doctor raises
my arm. He asks me about the sores

in my mouth and nose and eyes and about how
I urinate and eat and sleep. All this

is comforting, but metaphorical.
There is one cold wind that blows

continually away from me
that knows what I am dying of.

I wore orchid shoes

and blue jeans with rolled
cuffs. Still today was too brilliant for me
not to notice my hands are already old.
Where I walked was so temperate my lunacy

came back. Shingled hyacinths in low relief released
their petals' tints to the sun. Hyacinths haven't begun
to show here where I live alone on Anthony Street.
A half-year ago I was ruddy and baked in the sun.

This spring I worry that the thaw will come
here and craze the last lingering snow
glazing the clay between houses on one
side of the street one day too soon no

matter how long I prolong the rime of winter,
hoping for strength, remission, a quick cure.

The Defamation of Penelope

I must think of you more often than most,
    weaving away in a white dress all day,
    tall in your thoughtful beauty. How perfectly

you waited. How modestly you tore
    apart your work each night. How
    I failed you when I traveled with my husband.

And once again when I was traveling without him. Then
    I took my loose ends out of drawers
    and tried to unweave the myths

and mysteries that design our lives. So
    if it's my face on the backside of the fabric,
    Wise Woman before me, we have to worry

that our cloth is raveling. I never meant
    to undo us when I began to travel. Yet I've never met
    an Odysseus who believed me when I said

he could be worth the wait for me. I would have waited
    forever for one, but here's the joke:
    it's a short trip. Times

have changed but not the crimes.
    The more I travel, the more I ravel.
    I'm weaving now, staggering, really, and still

I keep on weaving on into the night when
    I'll be folded up and put away
  with you. It's true, fair hands

only fall to dust. Penelope,
    some women shed their names like skins
  to keep themselves intact. But first or last,

you and I are cut from the same cloth:
    I too loved once with all my heart.
  And nothing can unravel that.

What's Wrong with This Picture?

Some of my best friends are men,
and I have nothing against them. Why,
only this morning I woke
with my back pressed against the hard
cold wall by my bed. Alone, and with the peculiar
dehydration that follows the nights of drinking
too many intoxicating lies. So I fluffed
up my pillows, made a cup of strong
coffee, and crawled back under my down comforter
with my books.

I got to thinking about the way fathers lie
to daughters and to sons.
The way they make up answers to questions
they have no answers for. Then
they call the lie art
to justify their absence
of knowledge and their gift
for painting their way out of corners.

The children crawl in bed with their mothers.
Mother and child embrace and trace the contours
of each other's faces
with their fingers. Sky
is sky,
the mother says.
Blue stones are blue.
I will die and you will die,
the mother says.

So when the father comes into the room,
ready with his reasons,
he finds the four eyes turned full on him
and clear.
He turns into a lie.

He goes off to his room. He puts on
an old shirt. He mixes
peacocks, lemons, and rubies
on his palette and tries
to explain why he didn't just
take off his clothes, crawl into bed,
and put his arms around the woman and child.
He leaves them
together, wrapped in the future.
Then the man paints the all-time lie
of his solitude.

How Not to Die

Outside the deathhouses in Singapore
old people squat in the stinking street,
gorging themselves on durian, a fruit
reeking of berries and onions and farts,
that must be eaten without the sense
of smell as pain must be felt without memory.
I watch one ancient woman's lips curl

above a fortune in gold stars cut in her front
teeth as she crouches by a monsoon drain
clogged with durian peels and pink
funeral parade streamers. She eats the fruit
of her last harvest without smelling it, peeling
back prickly skin, gouging out flesh, sucking
seeds bare. Although this durian's tainted
sweetness resurrects the aftertaste

of a childhood as painless and senseless
as memory, she hasn't enough sense left
to remember tomorrow—and so she will die.
How do *I* get off this street unmarked
on my itinerary? I remember that once
I stopped in the dry vegetable stink
of 44th Street to paint a Presbyterian church
to save the drunks knocking back Four
Roses on the flophouse stoop nextdoor.
I learned names for several diseases and novel
ways to die painlessly, and left the checkered
church behind. I've also left tight webs

of hair in hairbrushes, hard, white
crescents of finger- and toenails, twenty-four
hard, white teeth, flakes of dry
skin sloughed off in winter, urine
in specimen cups, in woods, and creeks, and foreign
toilets, feces, blood, a placenta, two
hundred fifty-five unborn children, and refuse
to recall any of these. I learned that the way
to live is forgetting the past. And so
I follow the rattle of mourners'
tambourines, trumpets, and drums dwindling
away off this street beyond the hearing
of the ancient woman eating herself senseless.

Hunger

It takes all my sense to remember,
yet nothing takes me back as fast
as a sudden scent. For two weeks

I've struggled to make
$5 last. This morning walking to work,
I felt dizzy from hunger and imagined

that each falling, scentless snowflake
carried with it an aroma of cooking food.
The smells were so foreign I slipped

to a time in Bangkok when I lived on less
for much longer. Two of us waiting
for a stipend so we could fly

home shared a bowl of soup or fried rice
once a day. I became, with time, reconciled
to fainting in the hot sun.

But what those smells reminded me of most
were the nights when we were unable to sleep,
or read, or make love

because of hunger. It's not
just a gnawing in the stomach—after a few days,
they say, the body begins

to eat itself, first draining
the deposits of stored fat
from the buttocks and thighs and breasts

before it begins to eat away muscle. Then
　　　it becomes hard to stand or move as the thin
layer of fat that lies

　　　between the joints of each bone is sapped. So
　　　　you believe your pelvis and back are cracking
as your hips and shoulderblades move

　　　toward the empty spaces left. You
　　　　actually begin to shrink.
But that happened long ago. Sense

　　　fades in memory. I could argue now
　　　　that the hunger I felt this morning
was as serious as anyone else's pain.

　　　The difference between their hunger and mine
　　　　is the difference between the past and present:
Simple selfishness.

Something Egyptian

The floor is terra-cotta, the walls sand.
   Unlike the multitudes out on the street,
   everyone is fine here, thank you, fine.
The crippled teenage girl, the hairless man,

the one who has a hole cut in his throat.
   He holds a strange device up to his neck
   and speaks in hieroglyph-made-words.
The patients range about in bas-relief.

Once at the drive-in I saw *The Story of Ruth*.
   At six I knew the plot, yet was afraid
   that on the giant screen things would go wrong.
But, no, the blemish magically appeared,

and Ruth was led away to change her gown.
   I slip off mine and climb onto the slab.
   "You don't choose ' ˘, '˘ chooses you,"
the doctor tells me. But I don't tell him

how many times I've heard such words before.
   The therapists begin their ritual chant:
   "Couch angle six." "Open to fourteen wide."
"She has a ten line." There, see, a ten line.

A small red cut-out casts the laser beams
   across my body's pyramids and dunes.
   They align lead pieces above me. Chanting stops,
and I am left alone, lying in light.

How long am I left alone? It is a life.
   At last they help me down from my high slab.
   I gather my gown about my blemishes.
The crowd steps back—all of them are priests.

But I, among Egyptians, am immortal.

At Bay

I know next to nothing about farming
    but today was a lesson at Bay.
Tonight we took our plates outside and Scott
    bent the branches of the mulberry trees down
so the children could pick the overripe fruit.
    My daughter snuggled in Naomi's lap.

We finished work and dinner just in time
    to see the firefly concert begin, light
as the sound of Vivaldi coming through
    dusk from the house. We garbed ourselves in Scott's
grandmother's clothes—chiffons, sequins, feathers—
    and danced on the lawn. The fireflies kept time

with each other, exchanging their photic
    responses singly until each second
was a moment of light. These were not like
    Pteroptyx who light up the trees in Kuching
where another farmer with arms like Scott's
    plucked pomelo and fat nangka for me

to taste. His daughters killed a young chicken
    beneath the stilt house, while he took me
through rice fields, orange groves, and the kerbau's barn.
    During the meal, the farmer, speaking only
Chinese, used his chopsticks to toss the best
    morsels into my bowl. The fireflies there

play synchronically. Whole trees light up
    at once as if the trees themselves are the source
of light. Here today in the generous summer light
    we shared Naomi's bread, deer sausage,
and our brief night's dreams. So tonight
    I wrote this poem in grandmother's clothes.

                    For Naomi Jacobs and Scott Ruffner

Toward Ecstasy

Into the muscle of church wall
    a cell is built. Within
the anchoress recites her prayers.

St. Juliane has been here long enough
    to abandon the thought that she's admired
by her neighbors in their stalls. At night

her face is strange to her, looking back
    from the window to the nave. Her face has become
more than she remembered it to be, as in illness

small errors acquire the air of sins.
    She has learned the art of contemplation
and sings the *Ancrene Riwle* to herself.

Think oft with sorrow of your sinfulness.
    The brocade gown she wore into the cell
has been carried away by her servants.

Think of hell's woe and of heaven's rewards.
    After a year she turned her face to a wall
and whispered into her hands, "Juliane."

Her voice had atrophied in the gloom,
    but she had another sin to pray for.
Think how false is the world for all you're worth.

She became for all the world all the world
    to herself. Her hands on her own cheeks
were the hands of an adulterer, the hands

of the mason running across the smooth walls
  of the Bride of Christ, her vestry, her choir.
She thought to herself, "Solitude is heaven's bridge."

Twice it happened the sun declined at such an angle
  as to cross the church and enter through her small
window, catching her on her knees, illuminating her hair.

Her thought became the thought of all her nerves,
  of all her muscles, of her skin, of the white moons
of her nails, of the graying roots of her hair, rising

to mingle with the hair of the nuns
  filing into Mass, and with the hair of the ladies
and of their servants and of the ladies' children,

a threnody of golden hair deliquescing,
  the wings of a golden bird, a halo of hair,
a cold song, o death in life, descending.

So as I walk uphill alone and a little ahead
  of the others, the view is mine, the breeze
a breath taken away. This glimpse of city below

is like nothing on the map, is all uncharted
  promise gathered into the reckless beauty
of red-tiled roofs, rooks flying from gilded

cupolas of government buildings, pigeons hobnobbing
  on the square. Ahead the indifferent back of sky.
Down there two cups of coffee steam

on a balcony, a pool goes slowly green
　　with leaves and dragonflies, cross-hatched lines
of light play across its surface, and dusty children

dip their fingers in the Baie des Anges.
　　It happens all my best-loved cities are named
for saints or pagans; men know so little

of beauty and so adore themselves. If solitude
　　is heaven's bridge, I'm more than halfway there.
Juliane, I would leap and leap again—for all

I'm worth. Always it's this way when I
　　am so high the gleaming city below me
looks like heaven at my feet.

Waiting for a Hero

December now, and I have stopped going down
        to the sea to meet ships careening
    into the harbor. The smell of mud and blood
        rubs the loose-belted women

who come to meet men and their stories.
        I have imagined the blue swells of the Aegean
    rolling into the Mediterranean and on
        into other seas. They hold a ship

tight in the trough of each wave. Still,
        I am waiting for one to come westward,
    imagining so long the sound of oars dipping
        toward home (the whir of a helicopter

landing on the roof of the Burn Center, a jet,
        a car engine dying in the driveway),
    that I can refuse to believe
        in a storm at sea, in his sudden loss

of blood, of heart, imagining so long now
        that the men have all gone Latin on me.
    The new heroes leave lovers, leave wives and queens,
        leave women to imagine the journeys.

Women believe *beyond* the waiting, into the future,
        where men return in their ships, shinny
    down masts, stride onto the familiar shore.
        Women left behind think the moon

sheds light on this land, that land, their lands
        joined, that the sun never sets but rather
    travels from the tropics, from drooping orchids,
        from mountains, to ice, to villas

and stucco apartment buildings not yet built. Year
              after year, century into century, they smell
      the mud of battle dried on fatigues, fatigue
              and disease and other women. Salt

dries lips and stiffens the bristles of beards,
              salt of sea, sweat, sweat of longing,
      longing always for the return, the return
              that will undo all that waiting has woven.

One war gives way to another, and only heroes
              return to their lovers. *That* is what hero means—
      to long for return, to believe in the long
              hours past midnight when the moon rises

above it all, nights closing in around women's
              rooms, around my room, around women in night-
      dresses, women who go down to the sea or not,
              who know the various sounds of oars,

horses, cars, planes, a woman who one day
              realizes how loudly the kitchen light
      overhead has been humming after it's finally
              snapped off.

Salt Lake City: For My Daughter in Virginia
    on Her Sixth Birthday

The mountains fold in on themselves
        Such violence the world has undergone
to bring them into relief
                            They appear
impassable from here   jagged
monuments to boundaries and the ways
people have of getting by
                            On Sunday
I drove up a canyon road that labors
        between two peaks
                            I stopped
for lunch at Ruth's where the bees
        drained flowers
beside my table
                        Why do I never
keep flowers in my room
                            Farther up
I parked the car and got out
to walk around
                        Up there
there's still some snow and though
        the sun was hot it didn't feel
like late May
                        Last year
I asked another hiker the name
        of the flame-red tasseled
wildflower that grows there
                            She said

it was Indian paintbrush
        as if I should know

                     From the place
I always return to in the mountains
I can see the city
                     still
in the distance
                     I broke
six paintbrushes from their stalks
        and held them in my lap all afternoon
I brought them back down
        to the city just as the late sun flared
on the lake
                     I arranged the sheared flowers
the paintbrushes
in a vase
              I put them here

My Mother Was Waltzing in Detroit

In Bangkok it is already tomorrow and the altar
on Sukhumwit is strewn with garlands of orchids.
The hungry children, some with straw-colored hair,
plunder the debris washed up against stilt
houses pitched beside the canals of the floating
village. In the rice fields beyond, three
Buddhist monks carrying wooden beggars' bowls
flatten into cutouts as their saffron robes
dissipate in the pungent flare
of a perfect sun ascending into yesterday
when most of my friends are asleep here, reading
the dreams on the backs of their eyelids.
One is, like me, up early, still
working in the feeble glare of neon on Broadway
where men of burned-out blessings mutely hang

together, like the notes that blare
from a jazz club, outside the plasma center.
Still, a thousand miles beyond mercy for me,
my daughter shakes off vanishing dreams,
jarring her father and his latest lover awake.
In Clemson, an old friend is pulling a T-shirt
over one godson's head, and in Ann Arbor, my sister
cajoles another awake as she returns from work
nursing chronic alcoholics at the VA all night,
while my mother was waltzing in Detroit, unaware
of any difference that might be possible
between darkness and light. Other friends in Boston,
New York, and Ellsworth tug window shades open,
and analyzing the weather and the night's unresolvable

arguments, contemplate the steam from their coffee,
rising to meet the clouds converging in the Canary
winds sliding up the coast. In London and Oxford
acquaintances are just going to lunch at the Marlborough
Arms or the Half Moon, yellowed in the streetlamps
pressing back the fog. In Poland
they're watching the news, while distant
relatives I don't know further east, in a country
whose name has vanished with the discretion of wallpaper
roses in a familiar room growing dark, are washing
dishes or dropping coins in the till of a crowded bus
beating curfew. Tomorrow they will line
up at the understocked shops
like the vague countries beyond, where dancing has stopped
across borders as disputable as the fine

cracks mapping the ceiling above my daughter's head
that once brought her out of bed crying to me,
afraid they meant once and for all
the ceiling would fall in,
and that are as fixed as the same familiar lines
I worried about, disappearing above me
in the absence of light
in my last room in my parents' house.
Mourning doves call in
the first light of childhood when I thought the edge
of the world began where sight ended
when the overhead light was snapped off.
The sun begins to rim the mountains here, a red
scar healing the horizon. As if
a new day were beginning